OTHER HELEN EXLEY GIFTBOOKS IN THIS SERIES:

A Century of Criket Jokes   **A Tankful of Motoring Jokes**
A Bouquet of Wedding Jokes   **A Feast of After Dinner Jokes**
A Megabyte of Computer Jokes   **A Portfolio of Office Jokes**

Published in 2001 by Helen Exley Giftbooks in Great Britain.
Selection and arrangement copyright © Helen Exley 2001
Cartoons copyright © Bill Stott 2001
The moral rights of the authors have been asserted.

12 11 10 9 8 7 6 5 4 3 2 1

Cartoons by Bill Stott.
Edited by Claire Fletcher.
Series Editor: Helen Exley.

ISBN: 978-1-84634-244-8

Acknowledgements: Rick Braithwaite and Matt Myers: from The Dictionary of Soccer © 1986
Richard Braithwaite. Published by Cool Change Publishing, 1986. Extracts from Colemanballs:
published by permission of "Private Eye". GREN: from The Duffer's Guide to Football © 1986 Gren
of the "South Wales Echo", published by Columbus Books Ltd. Reprinted by permission of the
author. Nick Hornby: from Fever Pitch © Nick Hornby 1992. Reprinted by permission of Penguin.
Extracts from "When Saturday Comes": used by permission of "When Saturday Comes" magazine.
IMPORTANT COPYRIGHT NOTICE: STUART AND LINDA MACFARLANE © HELEN EXLEY 2001

Helen Exley Giftbooks, 16 Chalk Hill, Watford, Herts WD19 4BG, UK.
www.helenexleygiftbooks.com

A TOP SCORE OF
FOOTBALL
JOKES

CARTOONS BY
BILL STOTT

HELEN EXLEY®

"NOT LONG NOW, VICAR – JUST ANOTHER 527 AND WE'LL
BE IN THE GUINNESS BOOK OF RECORDS!"

Footymania

"Bill Shankly, the [late] Liverpool manager
... was once asked by an impertinent journalist
if it was true that he had taken his wife to see a
reserve team match as a wedding anniversary
treat. 'It's not true at all,' said Shankly
vehemently. 'That's a lie.' Then he paused and
added. 'It was her birthday.'"

from *Comic Speeches for Sportsmen*

Telltale signs that football's taken over your life:

- You camcord games of Subbuteo for post-match analysis.

- You refer to the settee as the "dugout".

JON NEWBOLD

"It's easy to spot a football fanatic – they can
recite the team members of every World Cup
winning side, but can't recall their best
friend's name."

MARIA DEL CAMPO

What is football?

"The rules are very simple, basically it is this; if it moves, kick it. If it doesn't move, kick it till it does."

PHIL WOOSNAM, US soccer promoter, on the rules of soccer

soccer: a game consisting of twenty-two skilled players, one impartial referee, two eagle-eyed linesmen, and one stupid ball.

RICK BRAITHWAITE AND MATT MYERS

"... football is a useful and charming exercise. It is a leather ball about as big as one's head, filled with wind. This kick'd about from one to t'other end in the streets, by him that can get it, and that is all the art of it."

FRANCOIS MISSON, (1697)

Dirty tricks!

"He'd no alternative but to make a needless tackle..."

PAUL ELIOT,
from Private Eye Colemanballs 7

"Football is all very well as a game for rough girls, but is hardly suitable for delicate boys."

OSCAR WILDE

"Football's a game of skill... we kicked them a bit and they kicked us a bit."

GRAHAM ROBERTS,
from Private Eye's Colemanballs 2

"Demolition is the province of those players who find footballs a bit small and fiddly to kick around but opposing forwards just the right size..."

DAVE ROBINSON, from "The Art of Wing Play",
in When Saturday Comes, May 2000

"Never go for a 50/50 ball unless you are 80/20 sure..."

IAN DARK, from *Private Eye's Colemanballs 4*

"GARY – YOU AND TERRY SPREAD IT AROUND FROM
MIDFIELD – JASON, I WANT LOADS OF DUMMY RUNS
DOWN THE LEFT WHILE, WAYNE, YOU AND DAVE SUCK IN
THE DEFENCE. PAT, YOU RUN ABOUT KICKING LUMPS OFF
ANYBODY NOT IN A RED SHIRT...."

Team spirit!

teammate: another person you have to dribble around.

RICK BRAITHWAITE AND MATT MYERS

"The new striker had a terrible debut, missing numerous goal-scoring opportunities. Afterwards, he ignored the glowering faces of his team-mates and said optimistically, 'Listen lads, I've a strategy to improve this team 100%.' 'Great,' said the captain, 'when are you going?'"

JENNY DE SOUZA

BALL: Striker's scapegoat.

DEFENDER: Goalkeeper's scapegoat.

GOALKEEPER: Defender's scapegoat.

MIDFIELDER: Everybody's scapegoat.

JON NEWBOLD

"The players suspected that the manager wasn't 100% committed when he had a Jacuzzi installed in the dugout and started refusing to travel to away games."

HORST WILHELM

"'Forget tactics,' said the captain in his pre-match pep-talk, 'just go out and try to avoid a humiliating defeat.'"

LISETTE FAVIER

"You've got to believe that you're going to win and I believe that we'll win the world cup until the final whistle blows and we're knocked out."

PETER SHILTON, from *Private Eye's Colemanballs 4*

Down with the ref

"At least the referee was consistent. He was bad all night."

GEORGE GRAHAM

"I wouldn't say the referee was bad but even his parents shouted abuse."

HEIDI KLUM

Four good reasons to become a referee:

1. You love football but can't comprehend the rules.
2. You have an overwhelming desire to run aimlessly around in the rain and snow.
3. You love the sound of verbal abuse.
4. You find it hard to make decisions and when you finally make one it's always wrong.

STUART AND LINDA MACFARLANE

Tactics

"I went down to the dugout to pass on some technical information to the team like the fact that the game had started."

RON ATKINSON

I wouldn't say the manager's tactics are naive but...

"... blindfolding the keeper to keep him calm during penalties just isn't working."

"... his 6-6-1 formation was spotted by the referee immediately."

"... putting the ball boy on as substitute is asking for trouble."

STUART AND LINDA MACFARLANE

"That's great. Tell him he's Pele and get him back on."

JOHN LAMBIE, Partick Thistle manager's ingenious tactic, on learning that his striker, Colin McGlashan, was concussed and didn't know who he was

JOHN MOTSON: "Well, Trevor, what does this substitution mean tactically?"

TREVOR BROOKING: "Well, Barnes has come off and Roecastle has come on..."

BBC TV, from *Private Eye's Colemanballs 5*

"THE NEW COACH LIKES TO KEEP IT SIMPLE."

With fans like these...

"A football fan went round to his friend's house, and greeted him with,

'Oh well, my team's just lost again.'

'How do you know?' asked his friend. 'We haven't even got the TV on?'

'Easy. It's full-time isn't it?'"

JON NEWBOLD

"NO, WE SHOULDN'T BE UP THE OTHER END – WE'RE REALISTS!"

THE FANS: Two sets of abusive referees.

LUCY VINCENT

"Three fans were standing on the terrace moaning that their team was losing game after game.

'I blame the manager', said the first, 'if he would sign eleven new players we could be a great side.'

'I blame the players', said the second, 'if they made some effort they might at least score a few goals.'

'I blame my parents', said the third, 'if I'd been born in another town I'd be supporting a decent team!'"

STUART AND LINDA MACFARLANE

Definitely offside!?

OFFSIDE: The Bermuda Triangle of the pitch, where "innocent" players are drawn inexplicably.

JON NEWBOLD

"Fair enough, he was in an offside position, but I don't think he was offside."

JIMMY GREAVES, from *Private Eye's Colemanballs 5*

"IT WASN'T OFFSIDE. I WAS JUST WAVING TO MY PAL."

The offside rule constantly baffles fans, players and referees – yet really it's quite straightforward! A player is offside if they are nearer to the opponent's goal line than both the ball and the second last player – except on alternate Saturdays when in addition the second last player must be facing in an easterly direction.

A player is not offside if they are in their own half of the field, or they are level with the second last opponent, or the player, opponent and referee form an obtuse triangle as perceived by an imaginary linesman positioned on the Celestial Meridian.

STUART AND LINDA MACFARLANE

The offside rule is there to attract to football people who can already explain how to play cricket.

MARK SLATTERY

Another boring game...

"Complaining about boring football is a little like complaining about the sad ending of *King Lear*: it misses the point somehow.... I go to football for loads of reasons, but I don't go for entertainment...."

NICK HORNBY,
from *Fever Pitch*

"A father took his daughter to watch her first football match. It was a little dull, to say the least, and the little girl piped up, 'Do Rovers ever score, Dad?'

'How should I know,' replied her Dad, 'I've only been supporting them for ten years.'"

JENNY DE SOUZA

⚽ ⚽ ⚽ ⚽ ⚽ ⚽ ⚽ ⚽ ⚽ ⚽ ⚽ ⚽ ⚽

I wouldn't say the team are negative but...

"... their only striker suffers anxiety attacks if he accidentally strays across the halfway line."

"... the only set piece they practise is a cunning pass back to the goalie."

"... cobwebs cover the goalmouths."

STUART AND LINDA MACFARLANE

Pity the poor manager

"I see Atletico [Madrid] just sacked another manager before the season has even started. He must have had a bad photocall."

RON ATKINSON

"All the team are 100% behind the manager, but I can't speak for the rest of the squad."

BRIAN GREENHOFF, from *Private Eye's Colemanballs*

"Don't ask me if it was a good game. It would be like asking a surgeon if it was a good operation."

HOWARD WILKINSON

"All managers know that a player's cost is inversely proportional to the chance of his being badly injured during his debut game."

MARIA DEL CAMPO

"Always aim to resign the day before you get fired for incompetence."

BEE CHOO LIM

"IT'S NOT CRAMP, BOSS. HE'S GOT BOTH LEGS DOWN ONE SIDE OF HIS SHORTS...."

Goal!

SCORING: When eleven men spontaneously start dancing, regardless of "injuries", whilst eleven others droop like wallflowers.

JON NEWBOLD

"His jubilation at scoring a goal was heavily disguised: he only performed three somersaults and a backward flip."

LUCY VINCENT

"THANK GOODNESS HE DOESN'T SCORE VERY OFTEN. WE'D BE HERE ALL DAY!"

"I don't think that players should be allowed to dance after they've scored without having been auditioned first. They shouldn't be allowed to lie flat on their back and kick their legs either. They need a proper choreographer. And there should be more kissing."

MICHAEL PALIN

"LOOK – THIS IS NOT A FASHION STATEMENT. IT'S A SIGN
OF UNDYING LOYALTY!"

Football fashion

"Inside the ground I sit down and start to list the hats I can see amongst the Dutch fans. I note down: orange cows, red, white and blue windmill, orange fez with bobble, giant orange Tyrolean hat, inflatable orange crown, orange Viking helmet, inflatable orange clog, two foot diameter orange tam o' shanter, orange baseball cap with giant inflatable peak, black-and-white Friesian cow-hide toppers with orange pom-poms... and then the game starts and distracts me from this important task."

HARRY PEARSON, from "High Times in the Low Countries", in *When Saturday Comes,* August 2000

You can always spot a football fanatic – their face is painted with their club's flag – even though they're out shopping.

SUSANTA GHOSH

If in doubt... cheat!

"The feigning of an injury for the purpose of gaining an advantage is contrary to the spirit of the game. In such cases the referee is at liberty to give the offender a stern warning, send him off, or even award him a penalty."

LISETTE FAVIER

"JACK DOESN'T UNDERSTAND THAT YOU MUST HAVE AN OPPOSING PLAYER CLOSE TO YOU BEFORE TAKING A DIVE...."

"I've just seen Gary [Lineker] shake hands with Klinsmann — it's a wonder Klinsmann hasn't fallen down."

RON ATKINSON, on Jürgen Klinsmann's alleged tendency to "dive"

May the other team lose

"There must be many fathers around the country who have experienced the cruellest, most crushing rejection of all: their children have ended up supporting the wrong team."

NICK HORNBY, from *Fever Pitch*

Phrases a true supporter will never utter to an opposition fan:

"That was never a penalty – our player dived."

"Although we lost 7-0 I thought the referee was extremely fair."

"Congratulations – great win. Your team were far superior."

STUART AND LINDA MACFARLANE

A fan's definition of a good referee:

- ⚽ The ref must be fair.
- ⚽ The ref must be consistent.
- ⚽ The ref must make correct judgements.
- ⚽ The ref must be able to stay in control.
- ⚽ The ref must award your team several penalties and give at least two of the opposition their marching orders.

JESUS GALINDO

Don't shoot the striker

STRIKER: Faultless, box-hogging layabout who only misses goal when he's fed a bad ball.
JON NEWBOLD

"When he's in a clear shooting position he's under orders to do just one thing – pass."
RON ATKINSON, on Carlton Palmer

"... if you're in the penalty area and aren't quite sure what to do with the ball, just stick it in the net and we'll discuss all your options afterwards."

BILL SHANKLY, to a struggling striker

"If there's football in heaven, let's all hope that God's not in goal."

LUCY VINCENT

Losers!

"One of our players had a particularly bad game that day, and was constantly barracked by the supporters... after the game, [the manager] immediately picked on the player.

'Hey son, the punters are all shouting that you're useless, daft and stupid. But don't worry son, you're not useless, daft or stupid. I am. I paid forty grand for you.'"

TONY HIGGINS, from *Great Sporting Fiascos*

"I thought you said he eats, drinks, and sleeps football?"
"Oh yeah, he does. He just can't play."

JON NEWBOLD

"They say that pessimists see the cup as half-empty whilst optimists see the cup as half-full. My team haven't even *seen* the cup."

JENNY DE SOUZA

Put your best guys forward

"It's important that managers select the right type for each position. Defenders must have the right attitude (so resentful at not being good enough to play in one of the more glamorous positions that they take it out on opposing forwards), midfielders must have the ability to undermine the referee's authority with the merest curl of the lip and centre forwards must have a cruising height of six-foot-four or above. Of course the best position for some players will be 'left out altogether'."

DAVE ROBINSON, from "The Art of Team Selection", in *When Saturday Comes*, May 1998

defender: a player whose primary function is to commit fouls outside the penalty box.

RICK BRAITHWAITE AND MATT MYERS

"The goalie is the thick-skinned member of the team, taking the blame for everything. He's so unpopular with his teammates that they won't give him one of their pretty shirts to wear. He has to make do with one of another colour. And he's also the only member of the team who doesn't get kissed when they score."

GREN, from *The Duffer's Guide to Football*

The Thinking Man's Game

"Chiropodist — a brain surgeon for footballers."
JOHN HUTCHISON

INTERVIEWER: "Did you underestimate them?"
BOBBY ROBSON: "No... but they played better than we thought."

from *Private Eye: Colemanballs 6*

"THE LAD WANTS TO KNOW IF HE'LL BE EXPECTED TO RUN IN SLOW MOTION FOR TV REPLAYS...."

"After five goalless draws the frustrated manager gathered the team together for a pep talk. Sarcastically he began, 'Those large posts at the end of the pitch are called goalposts – the object of the game is to get the ball between these goalposts.'

'Wait, wait,' interrupted their latest signing, 'you're way ahead of us. First of all explain to us what's a ball?'"

BEE CHOO LIM

"I'm going to make a prediction – it could go either way."

RON ATKINSON,
from *Private Eye's Colemanballs 4*

Armchair addicts

"Sir – Instead of the present ninety minutes... would it not be possible to decide the outcome of each World Cup match by the penalty shoot-out method? This would result in the whole event being completed in less than a day instead of the interminable month or so that it takes now. It would also ensure that my husband could do something more useful than lying sprawled out on the settee, can of beer in hand, watching the tedious stuff."

AUTHOR UNKNOWN,
letter to the *Daily Telegraph*

How to frustrate your partner during a televised match:

- ⚽ Ensure the stock of remote controls have dead batteries.

- ⚽ Show a sudden interest in the fine art of footballing. Ask about *everything,* in particular the offside rule.

- ⚽ Announce that there's no popcorn in the house.

JON NEWBOLD

Foul!

soccer ball: round object used by referees to entice players into committing fouls.

RICK BRAITHWAITE AND MATT MYERS

"Batty would probably get himself booked playing Handel's Largo."

DAVID LACEY, on David Batty

FOOTBALLERS REQUIRED: Applicants should have the ability to subtly bring down other players, yet deny all guilt when caught on five TV camera angles.

JON NEWBOLD

"In an amateur girls' 'friendly' one young player was blatantly kicking and punching all the other players – even those on her own team.

'Hey Ref!' shouted an irate spectator, 'Isn't it time you sent off that troublemaker?'

'I can't!', snapped the ref. 'It's her ball!'"

STUART AND LINDA MACFARLANE

"PULL HIS SHIRT? ME?"

"KEEP AN EYE ON LITTLE TERRY. WE DON'T WANT TO LOSE
ANYBODY IN THIS!"

Mud, rain... and more rain

"Two zealous fans, sitting cold and miserable on the terrace, were complaining bitterly that the torrential rain and severe fog was making the game really boring. They decided they might as well go and buy a hot snack and at least heat up a little. Just as they were about to rise from their seats they were interrupted by a police officer, 'You two should go home now', she grumbled, 'the game was abandoned half an hour ago.'"

STUART AND LINDA MACFARLANE

"There had been heavy rain all week and the pitch was a quagmire. Nonetheless the referee ordered that the match be played. Losing the toss to choose ends, the home captain turned to his goalie and said, 'Get your life jacket on Goalie – we're in the deep end.'"

NICOLE REUBENS

Save **us** from bad keepers

I wouldn't say our keeper is bad but...

"... he suffers repetitive strain injury from lifting balls from the back of the net."

"... he's the hero of the opposition's fan club."

"... during one memorable game he saved a penalty and six fans fainted."

JESUS GALINDO

"GOALIE WANTS TO KNOW IF HE CAN GO TO THE TOILET...."

"Our goalkeeper had a nightmare match, letting in five goals against our local rivals. When he left the stadium he put his head in his hands and missed."

JOHN HUTCHISON

The long-suffering fan

"Football teams are extraordinarily inventive in the ways they find to cause their supporters sorrow... they draw the difficult away game and lose the home replay.... They seduce you, half-way through the season, into believing that they are promotion candidates and then go the other way.... Always, when you think you have anticipated the worst that can happen, they come up with something new."

NICK HORNBY, from Fever Pitch

Murphy's Law for supporters:

- If you're 3-0 up with ten minutes to go you'll be lucky to hang on to a draw.
- If, in the first round, you beat the champions, in the next round you'll crash out 8-0 to a bunch of amateurs.
- Injury time is always longer when you're winning than when you're losing.

STUART AND LINDA MACFARLANE

"A City fan and a United fan were walking home after a derby between their teams. Tired of her friend's taunting the United fan snapped, 'Well, at least we're good losers!' To which the City fan retorted: 'You should be – you've had all season to practise!'"

JENNY DE SOUZA

"WHY DO YOU ALWAYS SAY THE GAME'S NOT WHAT IT WAS WHEN YOUR TEAM LOSES?"

Football 1, Commentators 0

"Don't tell those coming in now the result of that fantastic match. Now let's have another look at Italy's winning goal."
DAVID COLEMAN, from *Private Eye's Colemanballs 2*

Most annoying phrases used by commentators:
"Oooooooooooohhh."
"Just a little closer and it would have been in the back of the net."
"He doesn't miss them from there." (Said when a player scores, two inches from the goal line.)
JON NEWBOLD

"And Wilkins sends an inch-perfect pass to no one in particular."
BRYON BUTLER, from *Private Eye's Colemanballs 2*

"If I ever needed a brain transplant, I'd choose a sportswriter because I'd want a brain that had never been used."
NORM VAN BROCKLIN

DICKIE DAVIES: "What's he going to be telling his team at half-time, Denis?"
DENIS LAW: "He'll be telling them that there are forty-five minutes left to play..."

from *Private Eye's Colemanballs 2*

Money, money, money

"There was a time when the players' respect for the manager was unquestioned. Nowadays, the Boss squeezes oranges for them at half-time whilst he listens to their latest pay demands."
JON NEWBOLD

"As well as name, number and totally inappropriate brand name, there is a further item that could usefully be added to footballers' shirts. Space should be found for their weekly income.

The next time your star forward hoofs the ball into the stand when faced with an open goal, the [x K] on his shirt will tell everyone exactly how much he's being paid to achieve this."

DAVID SMALLWOOD,
letter to *When Saturday Comes* magazine

"WELL, I'M WORTH FORTY-SEVEN MILLION...."

Sure signs that the game's gone to his head:

- He came on to the pitch in a limo.
- He autographed his own shirt.
- He refused to head the ball in case it ruined his hairstyle.

LUCY VINCENT

"WELL, I'VE GOT NINE FERRARIS...."

What runs through the mind of a player taking the decisive shot in a penalty shoot-out?

Right?

Left?

Straight down the middle?

High?

Low?

Hard?

Soft?

Spin?

Did I switch the gas off?

Oooops – I wish I'd concentrated on that one!!

STUART AND LINDA MACFARLANE

"Roberto Baggio, the sublimely pony-tailed Italian who fluffed a penalty in the 1994 World Cup final shoot-out, once said that there is only one way you can guarantee not to miss a penalty and that is not to take one."

ANDREW ANTHONY, from *On Penalties*

The men in black

"The chief gate-keeper at the City football ground rang through to one of the directors and said: 'The referee has just arrived with two friends who haven't got passes. Can they come in?'

'No,' snapped the director. 'There's something fishy about them. It's a confidence trick.'

'How do you know?' said the gate-keeper, 'you haven't even seen them.'

'No,' admitted the director over the phone, 'but did you ever know *any* referee who had two friends?'"

PETER CAGNEY

I wouldn't say the referee was strict but even
the crowd were frightened to move.

SIDRA MALIK

"St Peter was challenged by the Devil to a
football match. St Peter said, 'We've got all the
best footballers up here.' The Devil replied,
'Yes, but I've got all the referees.'"

JOHN HUTCHISON

Footy forever

"The most stupid football comment ever made (allegedly):
'It's only a game.'"

GIOVANNI ANDRETTI

"I used to say to Don: 'I'll try and die on a Monday, so you don't have to miss the match on Saturday.'"

ELSIE REVIE, wife of Don Revie

⚽ ⚽ ⚽ ⚽ ⚽ ⚽ ⚽ ⚽ ⚽ ⚽

"Two football fanatics were walking to a match.
The first said, 'My husband has given me an
ultimatum: It's him or United.'
'How awful!' replied her friend.
'Yes, I'll miss him.'"

JENNY DE SOUZA

"Some people think football is a matter of life
and death. I don't like that attitude. I can
assure them it is much more serious than that."

BILL SHANKLY, attributed remark